John Tucker

Reply to the Report of the Select Committee of the Senate

on Transports

for the War Department

John Tucker

Reply to the Report of the Select Committee of the Senate on Transports
for the War Department

ISBN/EAN: 9783337174989

Printed in Europe, USA, Canada, Australia, Japan

Cover: Foto ©ninafisch / pixelio.de

More available books at **www.hansebooks.com**

REPLY

TO

THE REPORT OF THE SELECT COMMITTEE OF THE SENATE

ON

Transports for the War Department.

BY

JOHN TUCKER,

(LATE ASSISTANT SECRETARY OF WAR.)

February 27, 1863.

PHILADELPHIA:

MOSS & CO.

1863.

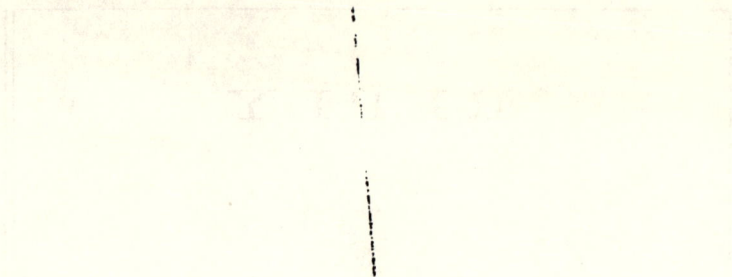

T O

THE REPORT OF THE SELECT COMMITTEE
OF THE SENATE

O N

Transports for the War Department.

B Y
JOHN TUCKER,
(LATE ASSISTANT SECRETARY OF WAR.)

February 27, 1863.

Hon. E. M. STANTON,

Secretary of War.

Sir :

I have only to-day succeeded in procuring a copy of the testimony taken by the Select Committee of the Senate on Transport Vessels for the War Department, on which their statements and conclusions are based. I preferred delay in answering the Report, that I might discover whether such gross perversion of the facts was due to the committee or the witnesses. In this answer I shall have occasion to quote largely from both the Report and the testimony. I believe the testimony of all the witnesses examined is a better vindication of myself than anything which can be written. I therefore invite the closest scrutiny and criticism of the evidence.

The serious facts, so far as I am concerned, presented by this Report, although not conveyed in the form of a direct allegation, are, that I have been guilty of a wasteful and reckless expenditure of the public money, and am a participant in the charters of transports during the period I was Transportation Agent and Assistant Secretary of War. I feel that it is due to the people of the United States, to you and myself, to answer these charges with the gravity becoming the character of the issues involved.

I shall comment on the various allusions made to

myself in the order in which they are introduced by the committee.

The first mention of my name is under the heading, "Charles Coblens and John F. Pickrill of Baltimore." Among the list of offences of the former, he is charged with being "a Prussian by birth, and an Israelite by descent, a peddler and a horse jockey by profession." Neither of these witnesses were interrogated with reference to any transactions with myself, except the general question put to all the witnesses, to which I shall directly refer. Yet in this connection my name is introduced with reference to the barge "Delaware," chartered for the McClellan Expedition at $70 per day. The Report states that these gentlemen subsequently became the owners of the vessel, which was entirely unknown to me till I saw their Report.

The committee, after exhibiting their estimate of the profits *for three hundred and sixty-five days*, the barge having been chartered *for only thirty days*, it being at the option of the Department to retain her longer in the service, observe: "That this chapter of fraud may want no odious and shameless features, Mr. Hall affirms, Capt. Hodges and Mr. Tucker thought she was the cheapest thing they chartered."

I may be permitted to express surprise that the Senate committee should quote and use the evidence of a witness they immediately proceed to charge with perjury. But I will apply *the facts* to the case. I will here remark, the intrinsic or permanent value of a transport did not control or even influence the price paid. This was governed by the efficiency or capacity of the vessel *for the exceedingly temporary service then required, viz:* Transportation from Perryville and Annapolis to Urbana, near the mouth of the Rappahannock river, a distance of about one hundred miles. By reference to the original record, I find the barge Delaware was chartered with a steam tug at $115 per day. The rated or estimated capacity of the service of the two was 1000 men, or 125 horses and 300 men. The Delaware was a very large, capacious barge, with three decks; she had been fitted, furnished and used for large excursion parties. It has never been reported she was inadequate to the estimated service. If performed, which I have no reason to doubt, I *now* assert that, *for the particular service required*, these were the cheapest transports chartered, although I do not remember ever before to have so stated.

The original record also shows, that the charter money first united in one contract was subsequently divided, and $70 allowed for the barge and $45 for the tug. I cannot remember that this was an act of mine, but as the services of the two might not be constantly required *together*, the separation was manifestly proper, and I will assume any responsibility connected with it.

2d. The next allusion to me is under the same heading. The committee, after characterizing the alliance between Cobleus and Pickrill as "nefarious," remark : "The only person connected with the government, who enjoyed the acquaintance of Mr. Pickrill before the breaking out of the rebellion, was John Tucker, late Assistant Secretary of War, who testifies that he has known Pickrill eight or nine years, and that he has had business transactions with him."

The question put by the committee to me was, "Have you ever had transactions with him in *years gone by?*" The answer was, "Yes, sir."

This business acquaintance, made eight or nine

years ago, I did not hesitate to admit to the committee, or now to readily own to the world. I could not, when before the committee, and cannot now, see the connection between that transaction and Mr. Pickrill's recent contracts with the government. The business with Mr. Pickrill, eight or nine years ago, led to much of my professional intercourse with you; hence no one is a better judge than yourself whether there was anything in it which was "nefarious," immoral or improper. We both *know* there was not.

The Supreme Court of the United States has just adjudicated the question, and decided it to have been at least legal.

3d. The next connection in which my name is used, is with reference to the charters with Mr. A. C. Hall, of Baltimore. The committee state:

MR. AMASA C. HALL, OF BALTIMORE.

Mr. Amasa C. Hall, of Baltimore, has played a very conspicuous part in connection with the chartering of transport vessels at that port. Hardly any vessel has been chartered there during the past eighteen months, that has not been secured through his agency, and of these earnings, from five to twelve per cent. has found its way to his pocket. During that time it has been understood among shipowners, agents and brokers, that no vessel could secure a charter of the Quartermaster at Baltimore, unless she was offered by Mr. Hall; and several of them testify that, knowing this, they were compelled, much against their will, to resort to him to do their business.

So singularly exclusive was the monopoly of this business enjoyed by Hall, that it at length attracted the attention of the Quartermaster-General, who called Col. Belger's attention to it by two letters, printed in connection with his testimony. Assistant Secretory Tucker's attention was also called to it more than once by Gen. Meigs (see Gen. Meigs's testimony,) but, neither of those officers seemed to have made special effort to correct the abuse. The evidence furnished by Hall himself in his letter to Col. Belger, throws much light on the otherwise intricate question of his monopoly. He says, " The Hon. John Tucker, Assistant Secretary of War, is aware of, and fully understands the nature of my business transactions with the Government as an agent for the owners and masters of vessels, and I would respectfully refer to him for any

information that Gen. Meigs, Quartermaster-General, may require."
This intimation seems to have put a stop to further grumbling, and
Mr. Hall went on as prosperously as before.

After commenting on the large commissions earned
by Mr. Hall, the committee remark :

It is no apology for either Mr. Tucker or Col. Belger for them to
say that they did not know, until a recent period, that such commissions were charged. It was their duty to exercise at least ordinary
care, attention, and diligence. They should have known, what seems
to have been well known by every man connected with the transport
business in Baltimore. They were bound to know the character and
the conduct of the man they intrusted with public business of such
magnitude.

Again :

The committee have endeavored to discover the motives which led
to the employment of Hall. He says himself that some one recommended him to Col. Belger as a suitable person to charter vessels :
but he is profoundly ignorant of the name of the person who thus
recommended him. The inference fairly deducible from the first fifteen pages of the testimony of Col. Belger would be, that this valuable friend of Mr. Hall was the late Assistant Secretary of War, Mr.
John Tucker : for Belger testifies that when he went to Baltimore,
he " went there a stranger, and Tucker expressed such confidence in
him (Hall), giving him those charters to make up, and he having
acted for Capt. Hodges in New York, I thought he was the very
man for me to employ. Capt. Hodges was the Quartermaster at
New York for that duty." It should be borne in mind, however,
that Col. Belger was totally mistaken as to the capacity in which
Capt. Hodges acted in chartering vessels at New York. He was entirely subordinate to Mr. Tucker, and only placed his signature to
charters already effected by the Assistant Secretary, for the purpose
of giving them an official sanction. He had no power to select, inspect or charter, save as personally directed by Mr. Tucker, and
acted in all cases precisely as Belger said he did in nineteen out of
twenty of the charters he effected, viz : as the mere clerical agent of
Tucker. Belger says that nineteen-twentieths of the charters he
signed were made " by Hall, by the direction of Mr. Tucker." When
it is remembered that, according to Belger's report, appended to his
testimony, the number of charters effected by him was 384, and that
nineteen-twentieths of these, according to his statement, were really
effected by Hall, at the instance of Tucker, though signed by Belger, an estimate may be formed of the magnitude and value of Hall's
business. If Belger's statement be true, not less than 360 of these
vessels were thus chartered by him, under direction of Tucker, upon
all of which Hall has received, is receiving, or is to receive, a commission of not less than five per cent. of their gross earnings.

Here is a labored effort to connect me with the daily current business of the Quartermaster's Department in Baltimore, and especially of that with Mr. Hall.

It is true, the Quartermaster General inquired of me why it was that Mr. Hall chartered so large a proportion of the transports in Baltimore. I replied to the effect I was not aware of it, and knew of no reason why it should be so. In the midst of numerous avocations and cares, the inquiry made no impression on my mind, as I did not then, and do not now suppose that the Quartermaster General regarded me as having anything more to do with the current business of his Department in Baltimore than in Portland or San Francisco.' I *know* you did not, and I did not assume it, as will appear by reference to the testimony of Colonel Belger, Quartermaster at Baltimore. His evidence is this:

Question to Col. Belger by the committee. Then your charters, which were made independent of Mr. Tucker, were also made through Mr. Hall, as well as those made under the direction of Mr. Tucker?
Answer. Yes, sir. I don't know anything about Mr. Tucker; but whenever I wanted a vessel of Mr. Hall, I would say to him, I want a vessel, and I don't want to go into the market for it; you go and pick me out such a vessel, and charter it at the lowest rate.*

The following simple narrative of my transactions with Mr. Hall, will therefore not surprise you, although were it not for my testimony and other evidence before the committee, I should suppose it would astound them.

The committee state: "Hardly any vessel had been chartered there (Baltimore) during the last

* The name of Mr. Hall does not appear in Col. Belger's Report as chartering vessels after the second letter of the Quartermaster General, who understood that the employment of Mr. Hall was arrested by his letters.

eighteen months that has not been secured during his (Hall's) agency." They then allude to the exclusiveness of the monopoly, after which they remark : " The inference fairly deducible from the first fifteen pages of the testimony of Col. Belger, would be that this valuable friend of Mr. Hall was the late Assistant Secretary of War, John Tucker."

The report is without date. It appeared in the New York Tribune on the 10th instant. I learn it was submitted to the Senate on the 8th, although a part of the evidence was procured February 9th. Therefore, according to the inferences of the committee, I must have introduced Mr. Hall to this valuable monopoly about the 8th or 10th of August, 1861.

The testimony reported by them proved this *utterly impossible.*

The committee examine Mr. Hall as follows :

P. 102. Question. When did you begin to have any connection with furnishing transportation for the United States army ?
Answer. I think it was in August, 1861.
Question. What was the first vessel you furnished ?
Answer. I cannot now state the first vessel ; my impression is, it was either the steamer Pocahontas or the Georgia.
P. 104. Question. When did you begin to act for the Government ?
Answer. In August, 1861, I think.
Question. How came you to be employed for this purpose ?
Answer. I have been in the steamboat and commission business for the last thirteen years. I was agent for a line of steamers in New York six years before going to Baltimore. Then I came on and took charge of the line of steamers from Charleston to Baltimore, and from Baltimore to New York : that was changed to the Cromwell's line of steamers. I was agent for them when they were first established, until the Government took the vessels, a short time previous to the time I have mentioned. Some one recommended me to Colonel Belger as being a suitable person.
Question. Who was that person who recommended you ?
Answer. I do not know. Colonel Belger sent for me to come to the office, and said I had been recommended to him.

Page 107. Referring to Mr. Hall's first interview with me, the committee ask him—

Question. How did it happen that you went to meet him in Philadelphia, or that you met him at Philadelphia?

Answer. Some time in the month of February, 1862; the first of February, I think, the Secretary of War, Mr. Stanton, advertised for proposals for vessels of different classes—different grades—steamers, tug-boats, and sailing vessels. I saw the advertisement, and I answered the advertisement, stating that I could furnish so many steamers, so many tug-boats, and so many vessels. Then I went to Washington, and there I met Mr. Tucker at Willard's Hotel. He was then, I believe, Assistant Secretary of War. I showed him the schedule I had. That was on Friday night. He remarked to me then that Captain Hodges and himself had been appointed a committee, or agents, to get up an expedition, and they wanted such and such vessels of such and such dimensions, decks, and capacities for carrying mules and horses, and steamboats for carrying troops. He wanted to know how many I could furnish, and I told him I could not tell exactly, but in a day or so I could give all the names of the different vessels. He asked me if I could get the information and have it so he could get it in Philadelphia on Monday: for me to meet him at his office. I told him I thought I could. I went home on the six o'clock train on Saturday morning, and went to work: got the names of the vessels; saw the owners and parties, and got the dimensions: and Sunday night I went to Philadelphia and saw Captain Hodges and Mr. Tucker. Captain Loper was there at the time. I had the names and dimensions of the vessels.

P. 109. Question. Do you know if any arrangement or understanding, tacit or implied, written or oral, by which you should be employed in preference to any one else.

Answer. No, sir. I do not think there was ever in the world any understanding of that kind.

The point which I wish to establish is, that neither Col. Folger nor Mr. Hall had any transactions with me prior to the McClellan Expedition, which was ordered by the President January 20th, 1862.

P. 117. Question. Did you charter vessels for them (Kelsey and Grey), for the McClellan Expedition?

Answer. I took vessels they had to come to them.

Question. Any for the Burnside expedition?

P. 113 and 114. Answer. No, sir. The Burnside Expedition I had nothing to do with.

(The Burnside Expedition sailed January 20, 1862.)

P. 130. Question. How came Mr. Tucker to employ you?

Answer. It was through this advertisement of Mr. Stanton's.

Question. How do you know it was through that?

Answer. I think it was through that, because I never saw Mr. Tucker in my life until I sent this letter in answer to that advertisement of Mr. Stanton.

Question. Was not that advertisement answered by other merchants, shippers, &c., in Baltimore?

Answer. I cannot say whether anybody answered it except myself, or not. I saw the advertisement, and took a great deal of pains to get the information, and reported to him. That was the only thing I know of that brought me in contact with Mr. Tucker and the War Department. It was my answer to that advertisement.

P. 164. Question. Did you charter any vessel for the Burnside Expedition?

Answer. Not any; only my two tugs.

(These two tugs were chartered by General Burnside at Annapolis.)

IN MY OWN EXAMINATION.

P. 342. Question. How many vessels have you chartered through A. C. Hall, of Baltimore?

Answer. I could not answer that without referring to that list; I am very confident that the first time I ever saw Mr. Hall was in Philadelphia. When I began to charter vessels for the McClellan Expedition he came to me and offered me a number of steamers; that was in February, 1862.

Question. Where?

Answer. In Philadelphia, at my office; it was the first time I ever met him, to the best of my recollection.

Question. Who introduced him to you?

Answer. I could not tell you now, sir; I do not remember.

Question. Did he bring any letter to you?

Answer. No, sir.

Question. Did you know nothing of him before?

Answer. No, sir; he had brought a description of a large number of canal boats—Schuylkill canal boats—and offered them to me at a price which we did not agree about. I had a fixed price for all I chartered—ten dollars a day. He demanded twelve; I told him I could not change the price. He went back to Baltimore, and, by return of mail, informed me that I could have them at ten dollars a day; I answered that at that price I would take all that he could get.

Question. Did you see him at the War Department before you saw him at Philadelphia at that time?

Answer. I think not; I have no recollection of ever seeing him until that occasion.

Question. You are confident that you did not advise him to go on and meet you at Philadelphia at that time?

Answer. Oh, yes, sir.

Question. Did you ever see him at Annapolis?

Answer. No, sir.

Question. Was he introduced to you by Captain Loper?
Answer. He might have been, but I don't remember it.

From Mr. Hall's testimony it would appear that my first interview with him was on the evening I left Washington, February 21, 1862, to charter the Transports for the M'Clellan Expedition, instead of the Monday following, February 24, 1862. When before the committee, I did not recollect that interview, and do not now. It was not such a one as would impress it on my memory.

(Page 346.) Question (To Mr. Tucker.) Your business at Baltimore was mostly done through Mr. Hall?

Answer. He came to me at Philadelphia with a list of steamers at a time when I wanted everything that I could get that was suitable.

Question. From that time on he has been in the habit of furnishing the government vessels?

Answer. Very few to me, sir, or through me.

Question. But to the government?

Answer. I do not know what he has done through the quartermasters.

Question. Did you give Major Belger any orders to charter from Hall?

Answer. I may have given some few orders to Major Belger.

Question. Do you remember the time when you gave Major Belger orders to charter vessels of Mr. Hall?

Answer. No, sir; I don't recollect having given such orders; although, if Mr. Hall had come to me and offered a transport which the government was in want of, and I knew it was a proper one and at a fair price, I may have directed Major Belger to execute the charter parties.

Question. Did you ever give Major Belger a general direction to charter through Mr. Hall?

Answer. Oh no, sir?

Question. Did you ever intimate to him that you would prefer that he should charter through Hall?

Answer. Most decidedly *not*, sir.

Question. Was the fact of the chartering of these vessels through Hall ever brought to your attention?

Answer. The quartermaster general has spoken to me of that fact; he did not understand why so many vessels were so chartered.

Question. When did the quartermaster general first speak to you upon this subject?

Answer. I think it was five or six months ago, in a casual conversation.

Question. How do you account for the fact that all the vessels were chartered through Mr. Hall at Baltimore?

Answer. I was not and am not now aware that that is the fact.

Question. I think it is pretty much the fact.

Answer. I had no idea of it, sir.

Question. I understand you to say that you never gave any order to Colonel Belger, or intimated any desire to him, that he should charter vessels through Mr. Hall.

Answer. I may have given him orders to charter a particular vessel; but I never expressed any desire that Mr. Hall should have any preference over anybody. That I am positive about.

Question. When the quartermaster general brought the fact to your attention that there were complaints about Hall having the chartering of vessels in Baltimore, did you take any steps to prevent it?

Answer. No sir; I did not consider it my duty.

Question. Had you not the subject of transports under your charge?

Answer. Not generally, sir.

Question. What was your specific duty in the War Department, or was it general?

Answer. It was general; but I was sent off in these emergencies.

Question. Would you as readily have chartered vessels of the owners as of A. C. Hall, of Baltimore?

Answer. Certainly. If you will refer to my report, you will see that the government advertised its wants, and directed them to apply, and preferred dealing with the owners.

Question. You know of nothing that Mr. Hall has done to entitle him to a brokerage from individuals?

Answer. I do not, farther than the owners seem to have employed him.

Question. Did you know that the owners had employed him?

Answer. I know in regard to these canal boats. I supposed that in regard to these canal boats that the captains employed him to represent them.

Question. If you knew that, why did you not charter them directly from the captains?

Answer. I would have been very glad to have done that, but they were in Baltimore, I was in Philadelphia, and the time was a most important element.

Question. How soon did you want them after they were chartered?

Answer. Instanter.

Question. Do you remember the day on which they were chartered?

Answer. No, sir.

Question. Do you remember how soon they were used after they were chartered?

Answer. I do not; I only knew I was extremely anxious to get them into service.

Question. How soon after they were chartered were they used ?

Answer. I should think within four days a portion of those barges were on their way from Baltimore to Perryville.

(Page 351.) Question. I think you testified that you never gave any direction to Colonel Belger to charter of Mr. Hall ?

Answer. As I said before, I may have done so in some particular case.

Question. You gave no such general direction ?

Answer. I have no recollection of it. I am very sure I did not.

Question. When it was brought to your attention that he was chartering vessels, and that nobody else in Baltimore was, you did not believe that you had authority to change it ?

Answer. That was never brought to my attention—that he was chartering all the vessels. I never was aware of that. My recollection is, that in a casual conversation with General Meigs, he spoke of Mr. Hall's appearing to be doing a very large business in Baltimore.

The Committee having referred to the testimony of the Quartermaster General with reference to the monopoly of the business in Baltimore, and my knowledge of it, I will give General Meigs's evidence on this subject in full.

(Page 294)   WASHINGTON, *Friday, January* 30, 1863.

Brigadier General MONTGOMERY C. MEIGS recalled, testified further as follows :—

Examined by the Chairman.

Question. Did you have any interview with Mr. Tucker or Mr. Hall in regard to the method of chartering vessels at Baltimore, or the persons with whom charters were effected ?

Answer. I have spoken with Mr. Tucker in regard to Mr. Hall being so much employed, or so many vessels being chartered through Mr. Hall, more than once. I do not remember any particular interview on this subject. I have told him that I had written to Colonel Belger upon the subject. Mr. Hall I do not remember ever to have seen, until I saw him one day in this committee room, lately, and was told, after he had left the room, that that was Mr. Hall. If I had such an interview it left no impression upon me as to its being of importance.

Question. Did Mr. Tucker, under the authority of the Secretary of War, have the general subject of the employment of transports under his charge during the year ending January 1, 1863 ?

Answer. I think that, during Mr. Cameron's administration as

Secretary of War, he held a position as superintendent of transportation; but I have not seen his commission, and do not know precisely what his powers were. I think he acted under the instructions of the Secretary of War. When Mr. Stanton took charge of the War Department Mr. Tucker was made Assistant Secretary of War, and acted in connection with transportation from time to time, under instructions from the Secretary of War himself; what his precise duties and powers were, I am not informed.

M. C. MEIGS,
Quartermaster General.

As the committee identify the testimony and transactions of Col. James Belger with Mr. Hall, I must also do so. Col. Belger, by the record of the committee, was the first witness examined.

The 2nd Question propounded to him was—How long have you been stationed at Baltimore?

Answer—*I was sent there on the 20th, May,* 1861.

Question—Did you charter any vessels for Burnside's Expedition?

Answer—No, sir; I do not remember that I did. If I did, it was by order of Mr. Tucker, the Assistant Secretary of War. I do not recollect now that I did, sir. I may have taken up vessels and chartered them by his direction when it was so stated in the order.

Question—Did you charter any vessels for the Port Royal or Dupont Expedition?

Answer—No, sir. I do not remember that I did, now.

Now, sir, I submit this evidence conclusively proves and establishes the fact that I neither knew, nor had a transaction with Col. Belger or Mr. Hall, until the latter called on me in response to your advertisement of 14th of February 1862, when I should have been derelict, if not criminal, in the performance of my duty, at a time when every suitable transport was required, if I had not seen Mr. Hall, with other similar bidders and competitors, especially as these transports were required in the immediate vicinity of Baltimore; and the Government could have well afforded to have paid even a higher price for them in Baltimore in preference to the delay and expense in procuring transports at distant places. If, then, I had neither seen nor known nor had a transaction with these two gentlemen until the last of February, 1862, which their testimony establishes, and which I solemnly affirm, I will leave it to you and the public to judge of the motive, the fairness and the truthfulness of the insinuation of the committee, that " the valuable friend of Mr. A. C. Hall, was the late Assistant Secretary of War, Mr. John Tucker," who secured to him this monopoly " so singularly exclusive," *seven months* before either of them was acquainted with me personally, or communicated with me orally, or in writing. I also aver, to the best of my knowledge, that from the time I parted with Mr. Hall in my office in Philadelphia, I never saw him, except in connection with the transports required for some rail road materials and machinery to be shipped from Baltimore for the McClellan Expedition, till the 27th of June last, and again once at the Department, and on neither of these two occasions was any business transacted, proposed, or even referred to. I met Col. Belger for the first time the same day in June, at his office. The next day he accompanied Gen Wool from Baltimore to Washington, and I went in the same car. On my return from Fort Monroe in September, on my way to Philadelphia, I called at his office for a few minutes (not exceeding ten). The next time I recollect to have met him was in the room of the Select Committee, to which interview I shall presently refer. I have not seen him since. Thus, to the best of my recollection, I have seen Mr. Hall but four times, and Colonel Belger but three. I concur with the committee that under any ordinary circumstances, " practically it is of no consequence whether Hall and Belger were brought together by

Tucker or not." But when the committee connect and identify the transactions as they do with " gigantic and shameless frauds," I submit, it is of "consequence," or at least it is so to me. It is further of great consequence as demonstrating the loose way in which the committee draw their deductions from testimony before them, and the reckless manner in which they make insinuations.

To recur again to the testimony of Col. Belger, and to my last interview with him. I called, as before stated, at the room of the committee on Saturday, January 31, 1863, by appointment, to read and sign my testimony. I found Col. Belger in conversation with the Chairman of the Committee, Mr. Grimes. Col. Belger advanced and met me with much frankness. I had not seen him for months, and was not aware that he had been before the committee. He at once said substantially this: " Mr. Tucker, I have been with this committee before, and on my return to Baltimore it occurred to me that I had unintentionally, of course, left an erroneous impression on the minds of the committee relative to our transactions, and I came from Baltimore expressly to correct it." I then, not having the most remote impression that any attack was to be made on me, carelessly replied, " Col. Belger, you must make it right; we want the exact facts. That is all." To which he replied, " I will have it all right." I was then requested by Mr. Grimes to retire until his interview with Col. Belger closed. On referring to his testimony on that particular day, I find these words : " I desire to append the " following documents to my testimony. They relate " to, and explain my previous testimony in regard to " the charge made against me of employing seces-

2

" sionists, including a letter from General Dix, ex-
" pressing his opinion ; also in regard to the subject
" concerning which you have inquired, of Mr. John
" Tucker's directions as to the chartering of vessels
" from Mr. Hall, *preceded by an explanatory note from*
" *myself to the chairman of the committee in which I cor-*
" *rect any misapprehension that may arise from my pre-*
" *vious testimony as to Mr. Tucker's directions to me.*"
The sentence just quoted (italicized by myself) closes
Col. Belger's testimony. The "*documents*" referred
to immediately follow, but the explanatory note from
Col. Belger to the Chairman of the Committee, in
which he corrects any misapprehension that may arise
from his previous testimony as to my directions to
him, *is entirely omitted.*

I leave it to you to imagine the reason for suppress-
ing this explanatory note. I refrain from commenting on it.

This "explanatory note" may have explained that
which is otherwise, to me, inexplicable. Col. Belger
and Mr. Hall have both testified they had nothing to
do with procuring transports for the Burnside Expedition (which sailed January 20, 1862), or for any one
previous, (except on one occasion when Col. Belger
assumes the transports for the rail road machinery
were for General Burnside, which was an error.)
For such transports as I engaged for the Burnside Expedition, and also such as he subsequently chartered
at Annapolis, I signed the charter parties as General
Transportation Agent. For those secured to move
Gen. Mc.Clellan's army, Capt. Hodges, Assistant Quartermaster, signed the charter parties, with the exception
of those required to remove the rail road machinery,
&c., to which reference has previously been made.

The reason for this exception was this. You well know that on the 10th of April, 1862, I was most unexpectedly called on by you to take important despatches from the President and yourself to the Head Quarters of General McClellan, near Yorktown. On reaching the steamboat in Baltimore, I remembered to have received that morning from Mr. Hall a note to the effect that the captains of the schooners and barges laden with the rail road machinery, &c., refused to leave until their charter parties were signed. Impressed with the importance that General McClellan's forward movements, (the necessity of which was so strongly urged in the despatches of which I was the bearer,) should not be retarded by any neglect of minor details too often overlooked, I, on board the steamboat (using, as it appears, the headed note paper of the Company) addressed to Col. (then Major) Belger, a stranger personally and officially, the following note, for a copy of which I am indebted to the committee.

BALTIMORE STEAM PACKET COMPANY,
Union Dock, foot of Concord street.

BALTIMORE, *April* 10, 1862.

DEAR SIR: I was *suddenly* called to leave Washington to go to Fort Monroe. I learn that the vessels loaded with engines and cars are ready to move, but the captains require that the charter parties should be first signed. Will you oblige me by doing the needful, as it is very important they should be ready to go on a moment's notice.

Yours, very respectfully,

JOHN TUCKER,
Assistant Secretary of War.

Major J. BELGER,
Assistant Quartermaster, Baltimore.

The committee endeavor to involve this hurriedly written note, or the words, "do the needful," in some mystery. I do not discover anything in either beyond the efficient discharge of my duty, and *I know* nothing more was intended.

The charters for these transports I did intend Col. Belger to sign. I presumed it was immaterial which Quartermaster signed them. The number engaged for this service the committee state was seventy-two. I may have requested Col. Belger at different times to have executed some dozen other charter parties for special purposes, although I cannot remember that number, and not one of them was taken through Mr. Hall. With the forty-five schooners, thirty barges, and sixteen steamers, the charters of which were signed by Capt. Hodges, and the seventy two charters of schooners and barges signed by Col. Belger, all chartered for the McClellan Expedition, in February and March, 1862, and confined to those two months all my transactions with Mr. Hall were included and terminated, *and all were the result of your advertisement for transports.*

So, also, with Col. Belger; with the charters of the seventy-two barges and schooners engaged for the transportation of the rail road machinery, &c., chartered in March, 1862, which charter parties I requested him to sign, and the possible dozen other exceptional cases during the year, his duties and acts were separate and distinct from mine. Any discrepancy between this statement and that contained in the Report of the committee, I must assume to have been explained in Col. Belger's "explanatory note" to the chairman of the committee, with a copy of which neither the public, the Senate, nor myself have been favored.

4th. I am next introduced in connection with Capt. R. F. Loper of Philadelphia. I do not propose to make any lengthy review of the comments of the committee with reference to this gentleman, except so far as they attempt to identify his acts with my own.

The committee state, page 17 :

The heavier operations of Captain Loper began with the appointment of Mr. Tucker as "United States Transport Agent," and they have continued, without intermission, during the whole of Mr. Tucker's two terms of office, first as agent, and subsequently as Assistant Secretary of War. Mr. Tucker employed Captain Loper to "inspect and recommend" all kinds of vessels at Philadelphia, New York, and Annapolis, for various services and expeditions, and Captain Loper proceeded to charge from five to ten per cent. commissions on the gross earnings of vessels recommended to Mr. Tucker for charter. In some cases it was denominated a brokerage commission, in others a commission for collecting, and in others still he received five per cent. for brokerage, and five per cent. additional for collecting the sums due to the owners.

I do not hesitate to assert these remarks are as entirely inconsistent with a truthful statement of the facts, as in the case of Mr. Hall.

Immediately after my appointment in Washington, in April, 1861, I returned to Philadelphia, and at once discharged such transports as were no longer wanted. Such as were best adapted and required for maintaining the line between Perryville and Annapolis, formed by J. Edgar Thompson, Esq., President of the Pennsylvania Rail Road Company, S. M. Felton, Esq., President of the Philadelphia, Wilmington and Baltimore Rail Road Company, and Captain R. F. Loper, acting as their assistant, were retained,

Of these there were a number belonging to transportation companies in which Captain Loper was interested. In every case the rate of pay was reduced. Many of these steamers were retained in service by different Quartermasters after the direct communication with Washington by rail road was opened, as they were peculiarly well adapted to the transportation of stores and munitions of war from New York and Philadelphia to Baltimore and Washington. They were expressly built for these routes. I regret that I have not statements before me which would show the exact relative price paid for these steamers, and any and all other charters made by any other officers of the Government. The Quartermaster General, in giving his instructions to Captain Hodges in reference to the McClellan Expedition, states:—

"For propellers and light draught steamers it is not possible to fix a rate. The offers received under the advertisement of the War Department, vary from fifty cents to one dollar per ton per day." *Those of Captain Loper's, to which reference is here made, are at* 41½ *cents per ton per day.* In addition to being so peculiarly suitable for the purpose, I believe them to be the cheapest steam transports known to the Department.

The committee state, " 'the heavier operations' of "Capt. Loper began with the appointment of Mr. Tucker "as United States Transportation Agent, and they "have continued without intermission during the whole "of Mr. Tucker's two terms of office, first as Agent, "and subsequently as Assistant Secretary of War." I will again test this statement by the facts never before so useful to me as now, in answering this report. By reference to " Senate Executive Document No. 37— 37th Congress, 2d Session," which was before the Committee, as they quote it, it appears that with the exception of renewing at reduced prices the charters of the propellers before referred to, I chartered from the time of my appointment as Transportation Agent, on the 28th April, 1862, to October 1st, 1862, but one bark (to take ice to Fort Pickens, an unusual service) and eleven propellers. These were all on special requisitions. The "heavier operations" began with General Burnside's Expedition. He commenced preparing for this movement about the 1st of October, 1861. After he had been engaged about two months in procuring transports, I was directed to assist him in obtaining any he might still require, and to expedite his departure as much as possible.

This duty required the purchase of a few steamers, as well as the charter of others, and also sailing vessels. At my first interview with General Burnside he informed me he had negotiations for the purchase of a steamer and a bark, which he wished to buy. He named the prices demanded, and the rates at which he supposed they could be purchased. He introduced me to the parties who offered them for sale. I replied I would have them properly inspected and would then again see the sellers. Before this inspection was perfected I happened to meet Captain Loper, who has built more steamers than any other man in this country. I inquired if he knew the steamer. He replied he built her and knew all about her. I then took Captain Loper to General Burnside to furnish the exact description, draft of water, &c., &c.

Captain Loper's valuation of the steamer was $12,500 less than the lowest price that had been named. He remarked he knew the owners perfectly well, and if it was desired, he was confident he could purchase the steamer at the price he had stated.

With General Burnside's approval the purchase was thus made. This introduction to General Burnside, and this result, naturally inspired confidence in Capt. Loper.

General Burnside's requisitions were peculiar and intricate. He required sea-going steamers, while he, of necessity, limited the draft of water to 8½ feet. He also desired steamboats to accompany his expedition, to navigate the bays and streams emptying into Hatteras Inlet, drawing less than two feet of water. It was difficult to meet these requisitions. I may properly inquire if such were met in other cases? They were in the case under consideration, and I suggest that much of General Burnside's success in North Carolina may be attributed to this efficiency in what may be regarded as minor details never to be neglected by a practical man in any capacity.

To successfully meet these demands, I availed myself of the great practical knowledge and experience of Captain Loper, who, from personal observation as a mariner, was perfectly familiar with every inlet on the coast, and practically experienced with every description of water transports from his early youth. How the duties were performed will be best stated in the following correspondence. General Burnside left New York in December with the transports he then deemed requisite. On his arrival at Annapolis, the place of rendezvous, he called on me for more. He also requested me to send Captain Loper to Annapolis to aid him.

The Committee again furnish me with this documentary evidence.

COPY.

Philadelphia, December 26, 1861.

DEAR SIR:—I am requested by General A. E. Burnside (by telegraph,) to ask you to go at once to Annapolis. You will oblige me by doing so and by aiding him in any way he may desire.

Yours, very respectfully,

JOHN TUCKER.

To Capt. R. F. LOPER.

Success is the standard by which the world judges. In this instance, it appears in the following communication :

ANNAPOLIS, January 7, 1862.

DEAR SIR : I beg leave to express to you my hearty appreciation of the services rendered me in the fitting out of the expedition under my command by Captain R. F. Loper. The interest and zeal manifested by this gentleman in this work has been constant and untiring, and he has in every instance fully answered every demand made upon his skill and his patience. I most cheerfully acknowledge my obligations to him, and take great pleasure in recommending him as a competent and efficient man, whose efficiency and mature judgment cannot fail to be of great service in any case of emergency.

Yours, very truly,
A. E. BURNSIDE, *Brigadier General.*
Hon. SIMON CAMERON,
  Secretary of War, Washington.

The committee next remark : " Mr. Tucker em-
" ployed Captain Loper to 'inspect and recommend'
" all kinds of vessels at Philadelphia, New York and
" Annapolis, for various services and expeditions, and
" Captain Loper proceeded to charge from five to ten
" per cent. commissions on the gross earnings of ves-
" sels recommended to Mr. Tucker for charter."

This refers to the transports for the McClellan Expedition. After my experience of Captain Loper's practical knowledge in the Burnside movement, and General Burnside's voluntary expression of opinion to the Secretary of War, " recommending him as a competent and efficient man, whose efficiency and mature judgment cannot fail to be of great service in any case of emergency," I did not hesitate to avail of such qualifications, when emphatically, time was money. I conferred with Captain Hodges, then sent for Captain Loper and informed him of our desire to avail of his services as an expert to inspect transports, that the Government would not pay him, and I wished first to have it clearly and distinctly understood that he should not receive anything in any form or manner from the owners or their agents. In short, there should be one exclusive and controlling motive, and that, the interest of the Government.

To this he readily assented. I then believed and now believe he was governed solely by this principle while he thus acted. I will again apply to the testimony to substantiate this statement. The first is from my evidence before the committee.

Question. Captain Loper was not receiving any compensation from the Government?

Answer. No, sir.

Question. Did you know the amount he charged the owners of these vessels?

Answer. He told me at the time that he should not charge them a cent, and has told me so over and over again since. In regard to that McClellan Expedition, he has never received a cent, directly or indirectly, from the owners; that was a condition that I made.

Question. Have you chartered any vessels through him since?

Answer. I have chartered vessels of him.

Question. Any through him, upon his recommendation?

Answer. I may, upon his recommendation.*

Question. Did you know what per cent. he charged for recommending them to you?

Answer. I did not.

The next is from that of Captain Hodges:

(P. 224.)—Question. Do you know of Captain Loper's receiving a commission from Thomas Clyde.

Answer. No, sir. I do not know of Captain Loper receiving a commission from anybody in the world.

(P. 230.)—Question. Do you know what consideration Captain Loper received?

Answer. I do not. I did not know that he received any at all.

Question. What did he represent in regard to his services?

Answer. As far as he was connected with us—Mr. Tucker and myself—he said he got nothing for it; that he was willing to give his

* It is here proper to state that after mature reflection, and an examination of the tables furnished by the committee, I do not remember to have chartered any vessel from Captain Loper, or on his recommendation after the sailing of the McClellan Expedition, for which fleet only four steamers at an average of less than $125 per day were taken of him.

services. If he could be of any use to the government, he was willing to do so. Mr. Tucker told him he was to get no pay; but wanted his services. Captain Loper willingly agreed to this.

Here follows Captain Loper's statement on this point:

Question. Mr. Tucker came on to where?

Answer. To Philadelphia. He told me that he and Mr. Hodges were appointed by the Secretary of War to get up the vessels for this expedition; but he told me that he was not authorized to pay me anything for my services, and I must charge no commission nor anything else for my services: I then told him that I would volunteer my services, and that I would charge the government nothing for my time. I examined all the vessels which I could find in New York and all we could get in Philadelphia; every steamboat that was fit, that could be taken, was taken. Mr. Flanagan, Mr. Groves of the Ericsson line, Captain Whilldin, and Mr. Clyde of the Express line, whom I had been doing business for, I told them each, and every one of them, that I could not take a commission in any form or manner, nor I never did take one penny for all the vessels examined for the expedition. We got all that we could get in New York. Since this war begun, I have been offered by almost all the ship-brokers in New York to divide the commission with me on vessels, which offer I never have accepted; not one dollar, either directly or indirectly.

(P. 267.)—Question. What proportion do you suppose your percentage as brokerage would bear to the aggregate amount that you have received for advancing and collecting money?

Answer. I never received anything in any other way than for advancing and collecting—not a dollar; I never have charged anything for interest in any case except that of Captain Whilldin.

Question. You have charged for advancing and collecting?

Answer. I have charged for advancing and collecting five per cent—only five per cent.

Question. In some instances have you not charged more?

Answer. No, sir; not one, with the exception of Captain Whilldin; I did not charge that; he gave it to me; that arrangement with Captain Whilldin was two or three months after the vessels were chartered.

Question. In no other instance than Captain Whilldin's?

Answer. Not that I remember of.

Question. If you had done it, would you have remembered it?

Answer. I think I should, sir.

Question. In addition to the commission, do you not get about five per cent. for advancing and collecting?

Answer. No, sir; the five per cent. includes everything, except in the case of Captain Whilldin; I did not charge one cent for advancing or interest. For Mr. Williams, of the steamer Patapsco, I advanced $75,000 for three months.

Question. You have received five per cent. from Mr. Reybold ?
Answer. Yes, sir.
Question. And Captain Whilldin ?
Answer. Yes, sir.
Question. And Mr. Groves ?
Answer. I have received five per cent from Mr. Whilldin, Mr. Flanagan, Mr. Reybold, Mr. Groves, and from Mr. Clyde, for part of his vessels. I gave up his charters last July.

The transports here referred to were not for the McClellan Expedition.

I respectfully submit that this evidence establishes the fact that on the transports I requested Capt. Loper to "inspect and recommend," he did *not* proceed to charge five and ten per cent. commissions, or any commissions whatever.

It is proper to state, that none of the vessels inspected or recommended by Captain Loper, or any others chartered by me, met with any accident while in the service for which they were chartered. I did not procure, or charter, or have anything to do with engaging any of the transports for the Banks' Expedition.

The next point to which allusion is made by the committee is the charter of the steamers Champion and Louisiana. I do not remember about the former. She was not chartered by me. With reference to the latter, "the committee regret that their time has not permitted an investigation into the facts connected with the charter of the Louisiana, which was taken into the Government service on the 8th January, 1862, at the enormous rate of $800 per day, and is still in the service. Col. Belger testifies that she was chartered by Tucker, and that he, Belger, has paid by order of the Quartermaster General, at different times $200,410.23 for her services for 251 days. But she has been in the service over a year, and there must be still a sum due her greater than her entire value." I was not questioned by the committee with reference to this charter, but will now give the facts connected with it. The committee state Captain Loper has sworn "she was chartered by Mr. Brandt directly to Gen'l Burnside without being examined by himself." The committee have before stated she was chartered on the 8th of January, 1862 This was the exact time when General Burnside was chartering vessels at Annapolis. He was in an emergency for transports. The Government were impatient at the delay in the sailing of his expedition. The daily expense by the detention was enormous.

General Burnside was most anxious to get away. He had found the transports, which he supposed sufficient when he left New York, inadequate on his arrival at Annapolis. He required more. The "Louisiana" was a most capacious and costly steam transport. He wanted her for a short time only. He could not tell the owners the voyage required to be performed, as his destination was a secret. Hence insurance was not to be obtained. The owners knew their steamer was not adapted to a long sea voyage, or very rough weather. Therefore the high price acceded to by General Burnside, and reluctantly accepted (as I am informed) by the owners. I knew nothing of the transaction at the time, but at the request of General Burnside signed the charter parties, as I did all the others he made at Annapolis. I learned the facts, however, a short time afterwards, when the owners informed me their fine steamer had been seriously damaged by being ashore in Hatteras Inlet, and they supposed they had an equitable claim for the damages. These were not allowed. The committee err in stating the "Louisiana has been over a year and is still in the service, and there must still be a sum due her greater than her entire value."

Colonel Belger states in his testimony, the "Louisiana" was discharged on the 15th of September, 1862, and paid in full. He adds he employed her four days from 4th of December, 1862, to 8th December, 1862, at $600 per day.*

The next reference to myself is in connection with Mr. James B. Danforth, of New York, and the steamer "Metamora." I have known Mr. Danforth for many years. Before I reached the city of New York, the telegraph had communicated to the country the demand of the Government for transports. Mr. Danforth, shortly after my arrival, introduced different persons (strangers to me) who made offers of transports, which after examination and negotiation, and a reduction of price in most cases, were accepted. These transports were among the very best that were procured, and fully performed all that was represented of them. I perfected these charters in every instance with the owners, not knowing or having the most remote idea that Mr. Danforth had an interest of any description in them. The first intimation reached me in the month of August following, when I was informed of it by one of the owners. I had no manner of interest, direct or indirect, in these steamers or charters, or in any interest Mr. Danforth may have had in them. I much regret Mr Danforth was not examined by the Committee.†

---

* The "Louisiana" was discharged from the department of Gen. Burnside in March, 1862.

† I learn that he waited on them at their hotel, in New York, and intimated his readiness to be examined.

With reference to the steamer Metamora, the Committee state :

Another extraordinary condition of facts is developed in connection with this steamer. She was an old vessel, and cost her owners $25,000. She was chartered by Assistant Secretary of War, John Tucker, though the latter gentleman has failed, for some unexplained reason, to include her name in the list he furnished to the committee, of vessels chartered by him or under his direction. The price paid for her by the government, was $450 per day. According to the testimony of Mr. Lewis Baker, one of her owners, "she was chartered to be delivered at Annapolis on the 6th of March, 1862. I state from memory. A telegram came on here from one of the owners in New York to deliver her there on the 6th of March, with 4,000 gallons of water on board. We got ready to run the blockade, and were stopped here on the night of the 4th by the Quartermaster's Department at 4 or 5 o'clock in the afternoon. That is the time she was chartered." * *

Question. When did your pay for the Metamora actually commence ?

Answer. We got paid from the first of the month.

Question. Why were you paid for that six days prior ?

Answer. That is more than I can state ; we were paid for her. * *

Question. Do you know of her having made a pleasure Excursion ?

Answer. Yes, sir ; we made an excursion on the 1st or the 2d of March down to a Rebel battery opposite Mattawoman Creek, called Cockpit-Point Battery.

Question. Was that on private account ?

Answer. Yes, sir ; it was our own boat; we knew nothing about Government then ; that was on the 1st and 2d of March. * *

Question. Those were two of the days for which you were paid by the Government ?

Answer. Yes, sir ; we were paid from the first of the month.

The evidence shows that the Metamora was not only paid for at least four days' services that she did not render, amounting to $1800, but she was repaired at the expense of the Government to the amount of $1447.02, and that during the time she was undergoing repairs, said by Baker to be fourteen days, she received her charter party pay $451 per day. A part of these repairs consisted of bunkers in which the private trading stores of some of her owners, who were army sutlers, were carried ; for it is shown that this vessel was used for private purposes, and that some of the owners realized upon one trip of the vessel to Harrison's Landing the handsome profit of $3,100. It is stated by one of the owners, Mr. John Packer, and also by Mr. John Tucker, who directed this large amount of repairs to be done to the Metamora (see his letter to Col. Belger,) that they were paid by the Government in consequence of damage done to her by the performance of extra-hazardous work in the early part of May, 1862, when she was required to cross in boisterous weather from Fortress

Monroe to Cherrystone Inlet. By reference to Major Belger's account of repairs done to her, it will be observed that the items are:

May 29. Repairing Awnings, &c.	-	-	-	-	$32 35
May 30. Joiners' work, &c., and materials.	-	-	-	361 10
May 31. Painting, &c., and materials.	-	-	-	281 82
May 31. Pattern Makers' work, &c.	-	-	-	1,148 04
Aug 27. Carpenters' work, &c.	-	-	-	-	2,623 41

It would be curious to know how the straining of this steamer in heavy weather rendered necessary the application of $281 82 of paint, or $1,148 04 of pattern-makers' work ; nor is it easy to understand the connection between the strain to which she was exposed in May and the $2,623 41 of carpenters' work expended upon her in August.

The above extract is the statement which originally appeared in the New York Tribune. The following is taken from the official report :

It would be curious to know how the straining of this steamer in heavy weather rendered necessary the application of $281 82 of paint, or $1,148 04 of pattern-makers' work. By reference to Col. Belger's report of vessels repaired at Baltimore under his direction, (p. 304,) it may be fairly inferred that the dates were intended to designate the times when the repairs were actually made, and not to the times when the money was paid for them, because there are many entries of repairs marked "not paid;" and these, like the others, are all provided with dates. The committee, curious to learn what connection existed between the strain received by the Metamora in May and the $2,623 41 of carpenters' work put upon her in August, addressed a letter to the Assistant Secretary of War, of which the following is a copy :

SELECT COMMITTEE ROOM, UNITED STATES SENATE,

Washington, February 6, 1863.

DEAR SIR : It appears from the list of vessels repaired at Baltimore, Maryland, under the direction of Colonel James Belger, quartermaster, which list was transmitted to me, for the use of the select committee of the Senate on the chartering of transports for the Banks expedition, &c., by the honorable Secretary of War, that the steamer Metamora received the following repairs :

1862, May 29. Repairing awnings, &c.	-	-	-	$32 35
1862, May 30. Joiners' work, &c.	-	-	-	-	361 90
1862, May 31. Painting, &c.	-	-	-	-	281 82
1862, May 31. Pattern-makers' work, &c.	-	-	-	1,148 04
1862, Aug. 27. Carpenters' work, &c.	-	-	-	2,623 41

$4,447 52

The committee desire to ascertain whether the last-mentioned sum of $2,623.41 was paid for work done on or about the 27th of August, or for work done on or about May 30, when the previous repairs were made on said steamer, there being nothing in Colonel Belger's report to show, with certainty, whether the dates refer to the time when the repairs were done and completed, or to the time when the money was paid for the same. Will you please inform the committee whether there is any record in the War Department to elucidate this point?

* * * * * * * * * *

Very respectfully, your obedient servant,

JAMES W. GRIMES, *Chairman, &c.*

Hon. P. H. WATSON, *Assistant Secretary of War.*

On the 9th inst. the Assistant Secretary of War, by direction of the Secretary, transmitted to the Committee the following letter from Col. Belger:—

QUARTERMASTER'S OFFICE,
Baltimore, February 7, 1863.

SIR: I have the honor to acknowledge the receipt of your letter dated February 6, 1863, enclosing a copy of a portion of a letter from Senator Grimes, relative to the repairs made upon the steamer "Metamora," and, in reply, to state that the date, August 27, 1862, which was placed opposite the amount for carpenters' work, &c., $2,623.41, on this steamer, was the date of the payment of the account. The proper date should be May 31, 1862.

Enclosed I hand you the order for the repairs of said steamer, received from the Hon. John Tucker, then Assistant Secretary of War. Very respectfully, your obedient servant,

JAS. BELGER,
Colonel and Quartermaster.

Hon. E. M. STANTON,
Secretary of War, Washington, D. C.

[Enclosure.]

ASSISTANT QUARTERMASTER'S OFFICE,
Department of Virginia, Fort Monroe, May 16, 1862.

DEAR SIR: The steamer "Metamora" was called upon to perform some extra hazardous service, in doing which she sprung her guards and otherwise strained herself. She will be sent to Baltimore in a day or two, for some repairs of her hull, rendered necessary by this service. It is the opinion of all the officers here who know the circumstances (in which I concur) that the cost of these repairs should be borne by the government.

You will please have her repaired *as soon as possible*, and returned here, as she is most useful.

Yours respectfully, JOHN TUCKER,
Assistant Secretary of War.

Major J. BELGER,
Assistant Quartermaster, Baltimore.

3

"It thus appears, that the August expenditure of $2,623.41 was
"really a part of the repairs of May 29, 30 and 31, when, as Mr.
"Tucker alleges, she 'sprung her guards and otherwise strained her-
"self.' The committee leave to Col. Belger the task of explaining
"the discrepancy between his two reports."

A portion of that which the committee did not understand, (the carpenters' work done in May, but not
paid till August, as explained by Col. Belger, does not
seem to be entirely satisfactory to the committee. I
will endeavor to make my explanations more so, although I had supposed my own testimony on this subject, which will be found in their report, pages 343
to 345, was sufficiently full and explicit, and to which
I ask reference.

The *exact facts* with reference to the "Metamora"
are these : The owners called at Capt. Hodges' office
soon after our arrival in New York, and offered to
charter this steamer. They stated she had just run
the blockade of the Potomac, and was then in Washington, where she had thus been sent to find employment. The steamer was well known. She was
chartered with others of the same owners, provided she was at Annapolis on the 6th of March,
1862, the time when the others, after being coaled,
obtaining supplies of water for the troops, &c., &c.,
were expected to reach that place. There was manifest propriety in making that condition, as she might
not again be so successful in running the blockade.
Of course she was then regularly entered on Captain
Hodges' list. The proper order was given by the
owners. The Quartermaster in Washington would
not permit her to leave. (See the evidence). The
owners promptly advised this result. Capt. Hodges
then erased the Metamora from his list of charters.
A few days afterwards Capt. Hodges sent me a state-

ment of the transports secured. Of course the Metamora was not on it. A copy of this list, prepared by
Capt. Hodges, (see my testimony) was handed to the
committee. It did not, of course, include the Metamora. You will remember that about the time Commodore Vanderbilt was presenting to the Government
his steamship Vanderbilt to destroy the "Merrimac"
(may I here say, resulting from my suggestions to
you) I was called on by you for the fastest steamer
at command, to send Mr. Vanderbilt to Fort Monroe.
In his presence I named the Metamora, then in the
service of the Quartermaster's Department. His comments about her speed and other good qualities caused
you to order that when she had performed the duty
then required she should be put on the Telegraph line
between Fort Monroe and the wires at Cherrystone.
On her being thus employed, and on application of
the owners, I soon after requested Capt. Hodges to
execute a charter party at the price originally agreed
upon. This is a fuller answer, made on reflection and
investigation, than that made during my examination
to the question put by the Chairman of the Committee, which I think could have been more appropriately
addressed to Capt. Hodges, who had charge of the records, minute details, and payments.

At this point, I beg to put the words of the report
on this subject by the side of my answer. The
Committee observe :—

"She was chartered by Assistant Secretary of War John Tucker, although this gentleman *has failed, for some unexplained reason, to include her name in the list he furnished to the committee of vessels chartered by him or under his direction.*"

Question. If you chartered the Metamora, how happens it that she is not entered on your list that you have furnished to the committee?

Answer. I think you will find on Captain Hodges's original papers, chartering vessels, that the Metamora was chartered and entered regularly on his list, and that a day or two afterwards the owner came to me and said that Major Van Vliet, or the quartermaster here, (Washington) could not release her, and that her name was, therefore, struck off our list; and subsequently Commodore Vanderbilt came here, just at the time he was giving the steamer Vanderbilt to the government, and some fast steamer was wanted to take him down to Fort Monroe, and the Metamora was assigned to that duty. It is possible that that was the first time I had anything to do with her, and that might have been the cause of the delay in signing the charter.

The Chairman of the Committee frequently interrupts a witness, puts his questions rapidly, expects immediate answers, is impatient at delay, and averse to explanations.

I supposed, however, the answer on this point was sufficiently satisfactory, as he immediately changed the subject (his practice) by putting the following

Question. Do you know anything about the steamer Highland Light?

If the explanation in my testimony why the Metamora was not on the list sent to me by Capt. Hodges, and the copy furnished to the committee led the latter to use the words that it was "for some unexplained reason," the foregoing additional statements will satisfy you there was no mysterious or designed *object* in it. Equally clear will appear the further references and explanations of the repairs, &c., to this steamer by the following statement :

While the Metamora was employed in the telegraph line, and at the time Norfolk was captured, the President, the Secretary of the Treasury, and yourself were at Fort Monroe. On the morning the Merrimac was destroyed you went to Norfolk, intending to go from thence direct to Washington. On your return you stopped opposite the Fort. I boarded your steamer, and was told you had sent an important despatch to the telegraph office, to go to Cherrystone. I remained till your messenger returned with the answer that it was blowing so hard, and was so rough outside, no steamer drawing four and a half feet water (the limit at Cherrystone) could live in the sea then running. You said the message was of great importance, and *must* go. I went immediately to the captain of the Metamora, and asked him to take it. He stated his fears that no steamer with the limited draught of water could live in the sea then running outside. I replied, the emergency was great, and if he could not go, I must find one that would. He answered there was no steamer better adapted for the service than the Metamora. He conferred with some of the officers of the boat, and then informed me that he and the crew would readily incur any risk, but he did not think the owners of the steamer would justify him in assuming such an extra hazardous risk ; but if the Government would pay any damage the vessel sustained he would go. To this I agreed. The message was duly delivered. When the gale abated the Metamora returned with her guards badly sprung, and some other damage had been sustained. The steamer was examined. I then, in pursuance of my agreement, wrote the letter (copy already furnished) relative to the repairs " *of her hull*," and added, " It is the opinion of all the officers here who know the circumstances (in which I concur) that the cost of these repairs should be borne by the Government." If any unnecessary expense was incurred for " painting," "pattern makers' work," &c., it was not by my orders, and I am not responsible. Afterwards application was made for pay during the time the steamer was undergoing these repairs. I conferred with the Quartermaster General on the subject. That gentlemen agreed with me that it would have been manifestly unjust to subject the owners to a loss occasioned by an extra hazardous risk, assumed expressly at the urgent request of the officers of the Government, and under a promise of indemnification. It was paid.

Here is Capt. Hodges' testimony on the subject:

WASHINGTON, Friday, January 30, 1863.

Captain Henry C. Hodges recalled, testified further, as follows: You asked me, when I was before this committee, in reference to the steamer Metamora being repaired at Baltimore. Capt. Acker presented me a certificate from Captain Tallmadge, Assistant Quartermaster of the army at Fort Monroe, of services by this boat. In this certificate Captain Tallmadge recommended that certain days, during which the boat had been undergoing repairs, should not be deducted from the pay of the boat, on account of service she had performed—extra service. I told Captain Acker it would be impossible for me to do so ; I had no authority for so doing. He then requested me to write to the Assistant Secretary of War, Mr. Tucker. I did so. I think I wrote two letters in reference to it. At last I got a reply from the Assistant Secretary of War, who said that he had consulted with the Quartermaster General and presented the facts to him, and that the Quartermaster General concurred with him (the Assistant Secretary of War) as to the propriety of paying for this boat, and directed me to pay for the time during which she underwent repairs, which I did. HENRY C. HODGES,

Lieutenant Colonel and Quartermaster, United States Army.

Thus I have explained why the charter was dated April 20, instead of March 1, 1862; the occasion which rendered repairs necessary, and that before ordering them to be made, I conferred with all the officers of the Government who knew the circumstances, and had their approval, and also with the Quartermaster General, before directing the owners to be paid while the repairs were being made.

But one thing remains to be explained, and that the allusion to the occasional use of the steamer by suttlers. I can only remark, if the committee supposed it was my duty to look to this, they mistook my duties.

If with this truthful statement, which is substantially in the evidence, any "extraordinary condition of facts" is developed in connection with this steamer, so far as I am concerned, I am not aware of it.*

I will not close this review of the Report of the Committee, and such of the testimony to which they refer, without alluding to some of the evidence before them, which they do not notice, but which I regard quite as important as much of that on which they so much enlarge, for forming a correct judgment or "conclusion" as to the motives, integrity and efficiency of an officer of the Government.

The committee do not refer to the evidence of Mr. S. S. Bishop, one of the gentlemen who was brought as prominently before them by my answer to their first interrogatory as was Captain Loper. Mr. Bishop testified as follows:—

Question. How many vessels have you chartered to the government?
Answer. I could not answer that question now.

* The Committee state, "that the Metamora was not only paid for at least four days' service she did not render, amounting to $1800," &c. I am informed by the captain that this is totally incorrect.

Question. To whom did you charter them?

Answer. I chartered to Mr. Tucker, when he was transportation agent, and to Captain Hodges, the quartermaster.

Question. Where was Captain Hodges quartermaster?

Answer. He was located at that time at New York, but was taking up vessels for the McClellan Expedition at this place.

Question. Who is Captain Hodges?

Answer. I understand him to be assistant quartermaster of the United States army.

Question. To whom else did you charter?

Answer. To Captain Boyd, assistant quartermaster of the United States army located here (Philadelphia).

Question. When did you make your last charters?

Answer. The last charter was made for a special purpose, yesterday.

Question. For what purpose?

Answer. For the transportation of coal from here to Washington and Alexandria.

Question. Who authorized you to make that?

Answer. Captain A. Boyd.

Question. State, if you please, the names of some of the vessels you have thus chartered.

WITNESS. Recently?

The CHAIRMAN. At any time—steamers and sailing vessels.

Answer. The steamer Beverly, a propeller; the steamer New York: the steamer Ironsides; the steamer Vim; the steamer Bristol; the steamer Anna Liza: the steamer Concord; the steamer Black Diamond.

Question. Are those all the steamers that you have chartered up to this time?

Answer. That embraces about all up to this time.

Question. Since the war began?

Answer. No, sir, recently: those are merely chartered for carrying coal and towing barges to Alexandria and Washington, under a ten days' charter.

Question. Have you chartered any sailing vessels recently?

Answer. None recently, sir.

Question. What steamers have you chartered previous to those you have just named?

Answer. I could not give you that information unless you would allow me time to answer it from my office.

Question. Is Captain Boyd stationed here now?

Answer. Yes, sir.

Question. Where you have chartered a vessel by the ton per month, what was the price?

Answer. The last was four dollars per registered ton per month.

Question. When was that charter made!

Answer. The charters made under Captain Hodges, or through him, were three dollars and a quarter per month.

Question. These vessels you have chartered, I understand belong to other persons.

Answer. Yes, sir.

Question. What was the rate of percentage you charged for securing the charter ?

Answer. The great bulk of these sailing vessels are owned in New Jersey. They are built there in shares of one-sixth, one-eighth, &c., and I charge five per cent. for securing the charter or freight, and for collecting it.

Question. How much did you charge on the steamers ?

Answer. The same rates for the sailing vessels and steamers.

Question. Have you had any difficulty in securing the payment of your charter parties ?

Answer. Only in waiting for the funds.

Question. Have you ever had any of them discounted ?

Answer. No, sir.

Question. Who are the principals for whom you have acted in effecting these charters, other than the sailing vessels you have spoken of ?

Answer. For the last steamers I have mentioned, the principals were R. F. Loper, president of the Transportation Company, and Thomas Clyde, president of the New York Express Company.

Question. Then the vessels you have recently chartered were for Captain Loper as president of his company, and for Thomas Clyde. jun., as president of his company ?

Answer. Yes, sir.

Question. Did you charge all of these persons five per cent. ?

Answer. That is what I expect them to pay me, sir.

Question. Why did Captain Loper and Mr. Clyde effect these charters through you rather than make them themselves ?

Answer. For the reason that I had employed barges to transport coal.

Question. Did you ever charter any vessel, or agree to return or pay to any person any portion of the earnings of the vessel ; have you ever agreed to pay any person or persons any part of the earnings of a vessel which you have chartered to any agent of the government ?

Answer. No, sir ; not as I understand the question—to an agent of the government.

Question. To any other person than the owner ?

Answer. No, sir.

Question. How long have you been in the ship broker business ?

Answer. I have been in it for my own account about twenty-five years ; I have been at it since I was fifteen years of age.

Question. Do you know of any advantage being derived by the government in chartering its vessels by private contract over the former method of advertising for vessels ?

Answer. The advantage in doing it by private contract is, that you have a better chance of obtaining the situation of the market than by publishing it.

Question. Explain, if you please, how that happens.

Answer. I will explain it in this way; if you advertise for a certain number of vessels, or a certain amount of transportation, you at once put up the rates of freight to all points from the market from which you are going to ship. But, under the system of privately securing the freight, you have a chance to feel the market, and govern yourself by the rates to the points where you are about to ship, and you get it at about the rate at which it is ruling the day you go into the market.

Question. Is it your opinion that the government has secured its transportation cheaper than it would have secured it had it advertised for vessels?

Answer. In almost every case, as far as my information goes, they have.

Question. Has government been able to effect charters upon lower terms than private individuals have been able to effect them?

Answer. In almost every case, yes, as far as comes under my knowledge.

Question. Have you chartered vessels to private individuals while you have been acting for the government?

Answer. Yes, sir.

Question. Have you chartered at higher rates to individuals than to the government?

Answer. Yes, sir.

The Committee did not examine Mr. M. S. Bulkley, who was also brought prominently to their notice by me, which I regret, as he, from my long official acquaintance with him, and the prominent part which he took in securing transports, was well informed with reference to the zeal and fidelity exhibited by me. Other witnesses (not referred to) were examined. Some of these had been in the business for thirty years, are chartering vessels to the Quartermaster's Department and merchants almost daily, but like all other owners, testify that they have not divided their contracts or commissions with any officer of the government.

I will here call your attention to the evidence of the witnesses on this particular point, and will furnish it in the order it appears in the testimony.

Mr. John P. Aker's evidence—

Question. I understand you to say that neither you nor your company have ever, directly or indirectly, paid, or promised to pay, nor do you hold yourself under any obligation in equity or law to pay, to any person, any sum of money or property in consideration of his or their having assisted you in securing a contract, or in securing favorable terms, of any description whatever?

Answer. I have not paid anything, sir, to any gentleman ; that is, no commission at all. As to the repairs on the Metamora, I will say this to you : the order was given for her repairs by the government in this way : she run from Fortress Monroe over to Cherry Stone Inlet ; she carried despatches for the government before the telegraph was laid there ; she made two or three trips a day across there ; it is a very dangerous place, boisterous and rough ; at one time she was ordered to go when no other vessel would go. Mr. Tucker was there one night, and ordered her to go out, but the captain refused to go. Mr. Tucker said the Baltimore despatches must go, and if the vessel was damaged, he said, " I will see that the government pays it." She went out, and she was strained and damaged. Mr. Tucker said, " I think it is no more than just and right that government should pay this expense. Your time shall not be lost, and she shall be repaired." She was only gone ten days, as the records will show. I employed a man last spring in Washington, for awhile, to see to my affairs there which I could not attend to, among other things, the Metamora, for which I paid some $200.

Question. Who was that man?

Answer. Captain Schultz. I paid him for seeing to the boat for a couple of months, which amounted to a few hundred dollars, and which I paid him. His name is E. Schultz. He was an agent which the company authorized me to employ to see to the boat. I did not call it the company. I asked him to assist me and see to the boat, which he was kind enough to do, and I made him a present of some amount. I think it was some four or five hundred dollars, along in April or May. I look upon that as nothing more than what is right. Some might call that a commission ; I do not. I asked him to see to our business, and he did so.

Question. State now, if you please, whether you as the ship's husband of the Metamora, or any other boat, or as the owner or part owner, paid any commission for, or reward, or promised any to any person for his services in connection with securing charter parties for you?

Answer. None at all, sir, except the money I paid Schultz, and to Mr. John Danforth, (meaning Jas. B. Danforth.)

Question. Was that the only money of the kind you ever paid?

Answer. Yes, sir; that and to Schultz.

Question. Or ever promised to pay?

Answer. Yes, sir ; and since I have not paid one dollar as commission on any of my boat or boats, that I am connected with.*

* It is to be presumed the remarks I made to one of the owners in August last, when I first heard of these commissions, stopped further payments. **Such would be the natural result.**

Question. Have you ever, directly or indirectly, paid, or promised to pay, any money or thing of value for the purpose of securing a charter, other than the five per cent. that you paid which you have mentioned? (To Captain Loper).

Answer. No; not one cent of money or any kind of present whatever.

Question. Have you ever, directly or indirectly, paid back any portion of the money you have received for a charter to any person or persons for the purpose of securing a charter party, or any other advantage in connection therewith?

Answer. Not one cent, sir.

Question. Have you ever employed any person or persons to secure a discount of a charter party?

Answer. No, sir.

Question. Have you ever paid to any person, other than Mr. Loper, any per cent. in connection with the procurement of these charters?

Answer. No, sir.

STEPHEN FLANAGAN.

Question. Did you pay to any person, any percentage for the vessels you chartered to Mr. Tucker?

Answer. None, sir, to anybody but Captain Loper.

Question. Did you pay to Captain Loper five per cent. for the vessels that were chartered to Mr. Tucker?

Answer. No, sir; those that I chartered direct to Mr. Tucker we never paid a cent for. I can enumerate them: the Atlantic is one: the Pendulum—she was lost in going from the Capes of Delaware to Fortress Monroe. Of course we never got anything for her, but we expect to up to the time she was lost; the Robert Morris, up to the first of April.

Question. Did Mr. Tucker send you to Captain Loper?

Answer. No, sir.

Question. Did he advise you to call on Captain Loper?

Answer. No, sir, not to my knowledge.

Question. Have you ever paid or caused to be paid to any person, any sum of money or other thing of value, for the purpose of securing your pay upon any charter party that was due you?

Answer. No, sir, never.

WILMON WHILLDIN.

Question. Have you, either directly or indirectly, in order to secure your pay for a charter, been compelled to employ any broker, or pay any percentage.

Answer. No, sir; I have not been compelled to; I have done it. I will tell you all that I have paid. I have paid Captain Loper a percentage for collecting my bills, and I have not paid anybody else one cent.

Question. What did you pay him?

Answer. I was to pay him five per cent. for collecting my bills. I paid him that, and I paid him at one time—a man might as well acknowledge his poverty—I paid him five per cent. for advancing me money. I had a debt of $30,000 on my shoulders. Government was owing that much to me, but I had to pay it then, and I had to do this. First I paid him a commission of five per cent.

Question. And then you paid him five per cent. more for advancing the money?

Answer. Yes, sir.

Question. Was the money which he advanced to you due on these charter parties?

Answer. Yes, sir, he advanced me money to carry on my business with.

Question. Was as much money due from the government to you on these charter parties as he advanced to you?

Answer. Not quite, but pretty near.

Question. How long was that advance for?

Answer. Until I got the money to pay him back.

Question. How long did you have it?

Answer. It was six months before I got it.

Question. Did he advance you this amount at the commencement of the six months?

Answer. It was soon after the commencement of six months. You see I went into very heavy expenses.

Question. Did you have Captain Loper's money for six months or for any length of time?

Answer. Some of it I had for six months; some of it I did not. I got what I wanted of it to carry my business on with. I had to meet the expense of putting the boats in very good order. I had other business too; this Express Steamboat Company I had on my shoulders made it necessary I should have the money. When I chartered these boats I said to him, " Captain, I want you to have the charters so drawn that I shall get my money at the end of every month. In that case I shall pay five per cent." He said he would, and the charters were so drawn, but the government did not pay one cent for six months.

Question. How much did you pay Captain Loper on the advance?

Answer. I told him if he would advance me the money I would give him ten per cent.

Question. And you paid him that?

Answer. Yes, sir; I want you to understand, however, that I was to pay him five per cent. commission.

Question. Was that besides?

Answer. No, sir: I said if I could get my money I would pay ten per cent. I did not want women (the wives of my men) coming to me for money and I not have it. If the government had payed me according to contract I should have payed him five per cent.; as it is, I paid him ten per cent. The paying of that five per cent., I think, is justly chargeable to the government not paying me.

Question. Are you paying Captain Loper any sum of money on the earnings of these vessels at this time?

Answer. Not one cent.

Question. On the charter parties now you are not compelled to pay him?

Answer. No, sir; I would rather pay him, because I do not understand going to Washington and collecting these things; I do not understand the routine.

Question. You employ and give him five per cent. to collect?

Answer. Yes, sir.

Question. That arrangement still continues?

Answer. Yes, sir; the five per cent. still continues.

Question. Have you ever been to collect any money?

Answer. Never but once, and then I did not collect anything. I was going down to Washington and had—I don't know what they call it, but I think an order or certificate of indebtedness that I got from Colonel Crossman here; I was going down to Washington with it. I had a cousin residing there. I gave it to General Spinner and told him that Captain Loper would be there to receive the money. I never received a cent except through Captain Loper, and I never begrudged him a cent, because, if he did not do it, I would have to run there and attend to it, and I do not know about these things.

S. S. BISHOP.

Question. Did you ever, directly or indirectly, through yourself or another, pay or promise to pay to any person, any sum of money or property for the purpose of securing you a charter?

Answer. No, sir.

Question. Did you ever pay to any person any money or anything of value for the purpose of securing you the payment of any charter party?

Answer. No, sir.

Question. Do you know of its having been done?

Answer. No, sir.

AMASA C. HALL.

Question. Have you made any agreement, or are you under any obligations in law or in honor, to divide with or pay any one any sum of money for assisting you in making these charters?

Answer. Not to anybody, sir.

CHARLES COBLENS.

Question. Did you ever pay or give any present or sum of money to any person who was in the employment of the government, for the purpose of getting him to aid you in getting a charter?

Answer. No, sir.

JOHN F. PICKRELL.

Question. Is any person to have, by any contract or agreement, express or implied, any part of the profits that you are to receive from these transactions with Coblens?

Answer. Not a cent, sir.

Question. Are you under any obligation, express or implied, legal, equitable or honorable, to pay any person any portion of these profits?

Answer. I am not, sir; such a thing has never been intimated to me.

CAPTAIN HENRY C. HODGES.

Do you know of any person in the employment of the government, either directly or indirectly receiving any money or valuable thing for securing or aiding in securing a charter party?

Answer. I do not sir; I never heard such a proposition made, and I have never heard of its being made.

ANTHONY REYBOLD.

Question. Have you ever paid Loper any more than five per cent.?

Answer. No, sir. Captain Loper knew nothing at all about the charter of the Tucker. He was in Stonington. The man I purchased her of in New York, told me the government offered him $500 a day for her. I don't know anything about that, whether it was so or not—only he said so. After I bought her, I insisted on that much a day for her; but Mr. Tucker said he would not recommend the government to pay that—that he would not recommend the government to pay over $300 a day for her. I felt that it was rather too low for a boat of her class. After the things were all fixed and settled, I mentioned then to Mr. Tucker that I was going to let Captain Loper collect her charter, as he collected ours; that it was a great deal of trouble to me, and I could not attend to it. I didn't understand it, and as he had collected the others, I would pay him to collect that. He said, " Very well." I did not say a word to Captain Loper about her charter until after he came home from Stonington. I then asked him if he would take it. Frequently along during the season, the boats were behind considerably in their payments, and I wanted money, and I went to Captain Loper, and he agreed to advance me money. He advanced me once as high as $15,000 on the charters. This paying five per cent. is all voluntary on my part. Captain Loper offered to give it up three or four months after the boats were chartered. I told him I would rather let him do it. My principal business is farming.

Question. At what time did he offer to give it up?

Answer. About three or four months after the first boats were chartered—before I owned the Tucker.

Question. At what time was that?

Answer. I should safely say, it was in the neighborhood of three months after the Express was chartered. She was not chartered until after the Whilldin.

With such an array of testimony, and from such answers by every witness examined on this subject, I submit it is not surprising the committee state " the testimony may not warrant the conclusion that any officer shared with him (Hall) the profits derived from his business." I think they might safely and properly have stated the reverse was established, not only as applicable to Mr. Hall, *but to all the other parties.*

The committee, when reporting on the charters of twenty-six steamers, *not made by me,* think proper to remark, " the terms of the charters of the steam vessels are understood to compare favorably with those effected with the Government in similar transactions." Eight of these steamers, which is as far as the comparison can be *exactly* carried, had been previously chartered by me for the Burnside and McClellan Expeditions. The prices paid in both instances were before the committee. On the occasions thus commended, to a certain degree, by the committee, the owners received *sixty-two per cent.* more than when they were chartered through me. It is proper to state, that in the cases to which reference is made by the committee, the owners were to furnish the coal for one steamer, and for twenty days for the seven others, and that in the meantime two had been rebuilt, somewhat improved and enlarged, but under no possible circumstances can it be shown that the prices which do not receive the censure of the committee were not fifty per cent. higher than those paid by me for the identical steamers.

It is in evidence that on my return to Washington, from my first visit to Fort Monroe (April 10th, 1862) on learning that it was the intention and policy to retain the transports for the McClellan Expedition longer in the service, (the propriety of. which was afterwards made manifest,) I wrote to Captain Hodges, not at the suggestion of any one, proposing a reduction in the prices paid to steamers chartered at $150, or less, ten per cent., all over $150, and less than $350, twenty per cent., all over $350 twenty-five per cent. I added, " you will please report to me the decision of the parties as early as possible, as it is intended to discharge at an early day such as may refuse to make the abatement."

The reasons for the proposed reduction are given in the letter which is appended to my testimony. May I not respectfully ask if such a letter would have been natural if I had had any other interest in these charters than that of the government; and also to inquire whether if the committee had desired to make a truthful impression upon the Senate and the public, they would have entirely omitted all allusion to this fact in their Report, which was prominently brought to their notice more than once by me, and also by other witnesses ?

If the Senators from Iowa, Maine and Maryland supposed that three hundred and eighty-nine transports, procured from all the cities and prominent towns from Portland to Baltimore, could be chartered and despatched in fourteen days (see Captain Hodges' testimony) avoiding and excluding ship brokers, they merely confess their want of familiarity with the usages of the world. The committee somewhere remark, it is no apology for me to say that I did not know Mr. Hall was receiving a commission.

Apology! I have none to make. I deny the insinuation that I gave to Mr. Hall, or any other broker, agent or owner, any preference. I know of no occasion for an apology. When Mr. Hall and other ship brokers offered their transports, my knowledge of the business of the world led to the inference (if I thought about it at all) that they were receiving the usual commission. To pretend anything else would be an admission that I was ignorant of an established custom. The evidence of Mr. Bishop shows, that the day before he was examined, he chartered a transport to the regular Quartermaster, on which he states he received a commission of five per cent.; and that a few days before, he had even chartered transports for the Government from Captain Loper on which he expected (as a matter of course) to receive the usual commission of five per cent. This establishes the custom, which is more general with sailing vessels than steamers.

I cannot, however, express my views in any more pertinent manner than I did in my report with reference to the McClellan Expedition, made to you April 5th, 1862, from which I here introduce the following extract.

All parties who offered suitable transports in reply to your advertisement had been requested to meet me. With few exceptions, such vessels were taken, and generally at a reduction from the bids. These, however, were by no means sufficient. As much publicity as possible was given, without further resort to the newspapers, that the government was in the market to charter vessels. In fact, with your advertisement and our action, it was notorious. Every owner of a vessel had the opportunity to deal directly with the representatives of the department. It was publicly avowed that the government preferred this course. When, however, a transport was offered, I did not stop to ask the party whether he was the sole owner, part owner, or merely represented the owners. Time being such an important element, it was enough for me to know (or I thought it was) that the party had proper authority to charter, that the vessel was suitable, and offered at the fair current price. To have refused suitable vessels till I could have ascertained who were the owners, or because they preferred to send an agent or even pay a ship broker, might have taken weeks, instead of days, to have secured the required tonnage, and also greatly increased the cost, by having a part of the fleet under charter waiting for the balance. I am induced to make these remarks in consequence of the objections which I have recently heard urged against the interference of agents or ship brokers. It may not be fully understood that in all great maritime cities negotiations for the sale, charter, and freighting of vessels are carried on, to a considerable extent at least, through ship brokers—a business class as firmly established as stock, land, money, or merchandise brokers. In New York they are well known as a class comprising many men of integrity and intelligence, whose services are not ignored by ship-owners. In France, Belgium, Prussia, and many other places, the charges for their services are regulated by a legalized tariff, from which the broker is not allowed to deviate. In Great Britain and the United States he is paid a commission, which, in the absence of a special agreement with the owner for whom he is acting, is regulated by custom and sanction of local chambers of commerce, boards of trade, &c.

In the case under consideration, however, no application was made to ship brokers, no commission tendered or asked, and no preferences shown. The wants of the government were made public. Every party interested had the opportunity of direct negotiation. The business was conducted with entire fairness to the owners of vessels, and with fidelity to the government. I beg to hand herewith a state-ment, prepared by Captain Hodges, of the vessels chartered, which exhibits the prices paid and the parties with whom the contracts were made. From this it is shown there were engaged:

113 steamers, at an average price per day of   -   -   -   - $218 10
188 schooners, at an average price per day of   -   -   -   -   24 45
 88 barges, at an average price per day of   -   -   -   -   14 27

In thirty-seven days from the time I received the order in Wash-ington (and most of it was accomplished within thirty days) these vessels were laden at Perryville, Alexandria, and Washington, (the place of embarking the troops having been changed after all the transports had sailed, which caused confusion and delay,) with 121,500 men, 14,592 animals, 1,150 wagons, 44 batteries, besides pontoon bridges, ambulances, telegraph materials, and the immense quantity of equipage, &c., required for an army of such magnitude. The only loss of which I have heard (and I am confident there is no other) is eight mules and nine barges, which latter went ashore in a gale within a few miles of Fort Monroe, the cargoes being saved. With this trifling exception, not the slightest accident has occurred, to my knowledge.

The custom of employing ship brokers by owners of vessels can be further demonstrated by reference to the immense business of the Quartermaster in this city. His advertisements for transports appear daily in the prominent papers here, and occasionally else-where. Yet I am warranted in stating that more than nine-tenths of all the charters he makes are through commission merchants or ship brokers, and that there is no difference in the price whether he deals directly with the owners or their appointed agents. The "Superintendent of coal shipments for the Navy," who is stationed here for no other purpose than to secure such transports, will also attest the latter fact. Custom has so established. In the case of the barges especially a ship broker soon became a necessity. Most of them were engaged by Mr. M. S. Buckley, before referred to, who made no charge *to any party.* They were taken at the close of winter, when their small savings of the previous year were much exhausted. The government made them no payments for three months. Many have been postponed for half a year, and in some instances even longer. In the meantime money and supplies were indispensable, for which an assignment of the charter party was an available security, and recourse to a commission merchant or ship broker the natural channel to procure relief. For these and other reasons, among which may be stated many of the captains were unable to write, (which appears in the tables in the testimony,) they, or most of them, soon applied to such agents to transact their business, make the necessary advances, &c. It may be asked why with these views did I exclude Captain Loper from commissions? The answer is clear and patent. I proposed to extend to him my confidence, to be influenced by his judgment in the inspection of the transports offered. It was therefore essentially requisite he should be entirely disinterested. He professed his willingness (as is clearly proved) to thus serve the government, of which I availed. But I am dwelling on this point longer than the occasion demands.

In this connection it may not be improper to state

that many of these barges were destroyed by fire by orders of the General in command, to prevent their falling into the hands of the enemy. Although this occurred in June last, no payments for these losses, although such risk was directly assumed by the Department, has yet been made.

Here I may observe, when thus acting for the Government in large transactions, fixed prices were established, after diligent inquiry as to the proper rate, whenever possible, without reference, as to whether they were made with the owners or their appointed agents. For the McClellan Expedition exact prices were made for schooners and barges, and although such an immense number was required and procured, not even one could now be chartered for less. With steamers it was impossible to have an inflexible law as to price, especially on the occasions when all that were available were required. As a rule they were chartered for only thirty days. It was not supposed they would be longer required. They were to be loaded to their utmost capacity with soldiers, many of whom were utterly reckless as to the damage and injury they occasioned, sufficient in most cases to render expensive repairs and refitting necessary before their ordinary business could be resumed. Many were engaged in regular and profitable trade, in well established lines, to be abandoned, never, in some cases, to be resumed. No owner knew how long his vessel might be retained in service, or on what day she might be thrown on his hands.

They were to be sent into waters with which those in command were not familiar. They were to be guided in narrow, crooked and shallow rivers by unknown pilots. They were to be under the directions of officers of the army, many of whom were inexperienced, while any disobedience of an order, however improper or even reckless to the property or life itself, exposed the offender to immediate punishment, and the owner to the loss of his previous earnings. Insurance, particularly on the river boats which were to make an outside voyage in the boisterous month of March, was enormously high. In some cases as much as ten per cent. a month was demanded. This on a vessel worth $50,000, even if chartered so high as $500 per day, would be one-third of the charter money. On steamers of very light draught of water sent to Hatteras even 33½ per cent. for the voyage was refused. Under such circumstances *minimum rates for ordinary service* should not be expected.

I will admit that had it been known these transports would be so long retained in the service, they could have been procured at lower rates. When this was known I made the effort before referred to, which in most cases was successful.

I now claim the right to submit some facts in connection with this subject which the committee have ignored, but which it is due to myself should be stated in my reply.

I asseverate that Captain Loper, A. C. Hall, and all the other parties to whom reference is made, or any of them, have never proposed or suggested to me in any manner to take or receive any interest in any charter or other transaction, nor have I received, nor do I expect to receive, from them or any other person in their behalf, or any of them, one farthing of the money they have received from the government or from the owners of the transports thus chartered.

✓I here repeat I had not the charge of the ordinary current business of transportation for the Quartermaster's Department; as a rule, it was only in great emergencies that I was called upon, the most important of which, were sending the McClellan Expedition to and from the Peninsula./ I need not now hesitate to state the exigencies under which I acted, and in forming judgment of my acts, these should be considered. During my first interview with the President and General McClellan, relative to the proposed movement by water, the time estimated as requisite was a serious objection with the President. At this interview, the President made the impressive declaration, that each day's delay was costing the country a million of dollars, and that every hour of detention was even more disastrous to the nation than the loss of the money. As the committee have magnified charters for 30 days into charters for 365, I may at least be pardoned for reducing the President's estimate of the results of delay to hours, $83,333.33, and even to minutes, of $1,388.89. *The entire cost* of the expedition *for a month*, the time for which it was chartered, was less than the President's estimate of the loss *in money* by delay for a single day. I therefore feel that in such an emergency, I need not further discuss whether the charter of the barge Delaware, with a capacity to move 1000 men at $70 per day, and the few other charters to which the committee take exception, were or were not wisely made. I have already stated the great expedition with which the movement was made. "The next prominent duty in which I was engaged, connected with the procurement of transports, was in bringing back the army of the Potomac. On the 18th day of August, a few minutes

after three o'clock P. M., I was requested by you to
start forthwith for Fort Monroe to expedite the return
of the army. I replied I could take the train that left
at 3½ o'clock. You rejoined, " Go, and make the whole
power of the War Department bend to bringing that
army away in the shortest possible space of time."
The General-in-Chief was present, and in order that
nothing might be left unsaid to impress upon me the
profound necessity for the strain of every sinew of the
national arm to effect an immediate movement of the
army, used this expression : "Remember this is a
great emergency, when every soldier you get here is
worth a gold dollar a minute."

I knew that General Pope's army was retiring, and
the enemy was moving to place himself between that
army and the capital. Under the pressure of orders
and facts like these, every transport then at Fort
Monroe, or which touched at that place, was chartered,
and others were ordered by telegraph to be sent there
in forty-eight hours. The result was, that in less than
six days, over 80,000 men were on their way to Washington, and within three weeks 27,500 animals, 2,600
wagons and the batteries belonging to the various Di-
visions, with the immense equipage of such an army,
were ready for offensive or defensive service at the
point indicated by the General-in-Chief. This again
was accomplished without the loss of a human life.

In speaking of movements of such magnitude, involving consequences so vital, it would seem to belittle
the subject to refer to inculpatory insinuations against
individuals, but as the fact is—so it must be stated—
that on this occasion not one of the persons who
are the subject of the animadversions of the committee furnished through me any of the additional

transports required for this service, or was in any way connected with the movement.

I fully recognize the truth, that in this momentous drama, involving consequences so grave, that the civilized world are its spectators, no one as an individual is of any consequence outside of the circle in which his interest and affections are centered. But when that individual from his official position represents by his acts and conduct, even to a humble extent, the administration to whose hands is committed the defence of the principle of self-government, he may then question the propriety of such insinuations and "conclusions," based on such evidence.

I remain sir, very respectfully,

Your obedient servant,

JOHN TUCKER.